I0163911

What Does God's Word Say About the Tithe?

McDougal & Associates
Servants of Christ and Stewards of the Mysteries of God

What Does God's Word Say About the Tithe?

The Secret of Your Blessings

By

Apostle Eddie Cude

**WHAT DOES GOD'S WORD
SAY ABOUT THE TITHE?**

Published by:

McDougal & Associates
18896 Greenwell Springs Road
Greenwell Springs, LA 70739
www.thepublishedword.com

McDougal & Associates is dedicated to the spreading of the Gospel of Jesus Christ to as many people as possible in the shortest time possible.

ISBN 978-1-940461-64-9

Printed on demand in the US, the UK and Australia
For Worldwide Distribution

Contents

Bring ye all the tithes into the storehouse, that there may be meat in mine house, and prove me now herewith, saith the LORD of hosts, if I will not open you the windows of heaven, and pour you out a blessing, that there shall not be room enough to receive it.

Malachi 3:10

Part I

Biblical
Principles
Concerning
Tithing

What Is the Tithe and Why Is It Important?

The tithe is important because it is the gateway for the believer into the covenant blessings of God. The Hebrew word *maaser* or *maasrah* is translated "tenth," or "tenth part," and the Greek word is *apodekatoo*. Both words signify "a payment or the giving or receiving of the tenth." The tithe is that tenth of our income that we give to God, which enables Him to move on our behalf in the area of blessings.

The Bible records numerous accounts of man tithing to God. God is the Creator of everything that exists. He owns everything, and we are simply stewards of what we have been entrusted with. The tithe principle is this; He gives unto us, and we give back to Him one-tenth of all that He has blessed us with.

Abraham tithed unto Melchizedek, Isaac tithed, His son Jacob and many others also tithed even before the Law was given.

Many Christians do not tithe because they have been taught that they are not under the Law, but under grace. While this is a true statement, God did not institute the tithe to bring us under the Law, but to get blessings to His children. Abraham tithed before the Law, and God blessed him supernaturally. We're under grace that we might establish the Law, not turn from it. Jesus said that He

11

didn't come to do away with the Law, but to fulfill it. Because He fulfilled it, we are to establish it. His Words are forever settled in Heaven, therefore we establish His Words upon the Earth:

Think not that I am come to destroy the law, or the prophets: I am not come to destroy, but to fulfil. For verily I say unto you, Till heaven and earth pass, one jot or one tittle shall in no wise pass from the law, till all be fulfilled. Whosoever therefore shall break one of these least commandments, and shall teach men so, he shall be called the least in the kingdom of heaven: but whosoever shall do and teach them, the same shall be called great in the kingdom of heaven. Matthew 5:17-19

— 2 —

Tithing Under the Law of Moses

And all the tithe of the land, whether of the seed of the land, or of the fruit of the tree, is the Lord's: it is holy unto the Lord. Leviticus 27:30

This scripture states that all the tithe, whether it be seed of the land, fruit of the tree, or one tenth of all that you earn, is holy unto the Lord. Never forget that.

Deuteronomy 14:22-29 states that one tenth of all that comes into our possession, in whatever form, belongs to God. This was God's plan from the beginning, to present His people a way of blessings that He had for them.

God is a multiplier by nature, and He could not multiply that which was not entrusted to Him. When the children of Israel were obedient to give back to God that which was His, increase for them was guaranteed.

The Scriptures state that it is better to be obedient than to sacrifice:

And Samuel said, Hath the Lord as great delight in burnt offerings and sacrifices, as in obeying the voice of the Lord? Behold, to obey is better than sacrifice, and to hearken than the fat of rams.

1 Samuel 15:22

When the children of Israel were obedient, blessings came; when they were disobedient, they had to sacrifice.

Today many Christians want God to honor the covenant He has made with His children, but disobedient children cannot receive the same reward as the obedient. A chain is only as strong as its weakest link. When we fail to tithe, we become that weak link.

Statistics show that only about twenty percent of Christians tithe. This means that eighty percent of Christendom is not in covenant with their God. They are, therefore, like beggars and thieves looking for handouts and what they can steal from Him.

I have said many times that it would be better to rob the First National Bank than to rob the Bank of Heaven. I'm sure most Christians don't see it as robbery, but the majority of Christians do steal from God. Malachi 3:8 asks an important question:

Will a man rob God? Yet ye have robbed me. But ye say, Wherein have we robbed thee? In tithes and offerings. Ye are cursed with a curse: for ye have robbed me, even this whole nation.

19

Wow! These are teachings that every Christian needs to know and obey.

— 3 —

Other Biblical Tithes

The Old Testament records two other tithes. One of these tithes was called the "festival tithe." This tithe was given when the people traveled to Jerusalem once every three years for fellowship, and it covered the expenses for that festival.

The third tithe was given in the third year and was, again, a tithe holy unto the Lord. The purpose of it was providing alms for the poor and needy. All of these tithes were brought to the central storehouse, and the priests over-saw their distribution.

The first tithe was for the up-keep of the priests. Since they had no physical inheritance, their income had to be derived from the gifts of the rest of God's people. This tithe, however, in and of itself, was never consid-ered to be an offering. Rather, it was the minimum requirement for all of God's people.

The reason God instituted the second and the third tithe through Moses was that His children needed to give above and beyond the first tithe. It was these tithes that God was referring to in Malachi 3:8 when He said people had robbed Him and had done it *"in tithes and offerings."*

In verse 10 of Malachi 3, you will notice that it states:

Bring ye all the tithes into the storehouse, that there may be meat in mine house, and prove me now herewith, saith the

Lord of hosts, if I will not open you the windows of heaven, and pour you out a blessing, that there shall not be room enough to receive it.

I am convinced that once people see the tithe as an instrument of blessing, they will no longer be looking for a way to avoid it or give less, but, instead, will want to give even more. When this is our attitude, God will help us to be generous on every occasion.

— 4 —

Tithing Establishes the Law

Tithing after the Law does not do away with the Law, but, rather, establishes it. Are you honestly blessed to the point that you can give generously on every occasion? Or are you like so many who cannot give the way they would like to be able to give? I've come to the knowledge that most Christians are looking for the truth, so they can be set free.

Just because you are a child of God does not mean you are a mature son of God. A mature son or daughter of God would never be found robbing their Daddy, God.

Revelation 3:18 gives us good counsel on how to re-establish right covenant with the Lord. There Jesus advises those of us who have become lukewarm to *"buy"* from Him gold that has been refined in the fire. And He tells us to do this so that the

shame of our nakedness will not
be revealed:

> *I counsel thee to buy of me gold
> tried in the fire, that thou may-
> est be rich; and white raiment,
> that thou mayest be clothed,
> and that the shame of thy
> nakedness do not appear; and
> anoint thine eyes with eyesalve,
> that thou mayest see.*
>
> Revelation 3:18

How do we buy gold from
the Lord? Hebrews 1:7 states
that His ministers are as *"flames
of fire."* In Matthew 25:9, Jesus

27

makes the statement concerning the five foolish virgins that they should go and buy from those who sell. What these virgins needed to buy was oil, and oil symbolizes the Holy Spirit.

Those who are in the five-fold ministry (apostles, prophets, pastors, evangelists and teachers) have a command from the Lord to receive tithes (see Hebrews 7). These tithes are not given, but paid, because the tithe belongs to the Lord. According to Malachi 3:10, we are to bring those tithes to the storehouse, and the storehouse is where we are being fed spiritually. So we are to give where we are being fed.

Malachi 3:3 states that the Lord will sit as a Refiner, purifying the sons of Levi (those in the ministry), purging them as gold and silver, that they may offer to the Lord an offering in righteousness. I repeat, Jesus did not come to do away with the Law, but to fulfill it. Our job is to establish it.

There are those who say that the tithe is not covered in the New Testament, but in Hebrews 5, 6 and 7, one of the main subjects spoken of is the tithe — who receives it and how to become mature through paying it.

In Hebrews 5:11-14, for instance, it states:

> ... *that you've become dull of hearing and that you should be teaching the first principles, but instead you have need of milk, and not solid food. For everyone who partakes only of milk is unskilled in the Word of righteousness, for he is a baby.*

This is preceded by the statement that Christ Himself has become our High Priest after the order of Melchizedek. Then, in Chapter 6, it goes on to state that once you have been enlightened and tasted of the heavenly gift, once you have become partakers of the Holy Spirit and have tasted the good Word of God, if you still fall away it is impossible to be renewed again to repentance, seeing that you crucify again for yourselves the Son of God and put Him to an open shame.

What is this good Word of God? This Word is *rhema*, which means, the spoken or revealed Word of God. His Word has been revealed to you concerning Jesus as High Priest after the order of Melchizedek, meaning that Jesus has become High Priest over the tithe, and over your life forever (see verse 20).

Chapter 6 further states (vs. 9-19), that God blessed Abraham by saying:

With blessings, I will bless you, and multiplying I will multiply you.

God also promised the immutability (unchangeableness) of His counsel and confirmed it by swearing an oath that by these unchangeable things, we might have strong consolation and lay hold of the hope set before us.

Verse 19 states that this hope we have is an anchor for our soul (mind), both sure and steadfast. I am convinced that these two unchangeable things are both God's promise to bless us and our promise to tithe back to Him.

Chapter 7 states, in verse 8:

Here mortal men receive tithes, but there He receives them of whom it is witnessed, that He lives.

Chapters 5-7 deal with the ministry of Melchizedek and that Jesus is the High Priest forever, according to Melchizedek. We know that Abraham gave tithes of all that he possessed. We know that in the Law of Moses, tithes were commanded. Then, after the Law, Hebrews states that Jesus is the Lord, not just of the past, and not just of the present, but forever. Hallelujah! He is the Lord of the tithe forever.

Seeing that Jesus is the Lord of the tithe, is He our lord? If He is, there should be no question that we tithe unto Him. I can just hear someone saying: "If Jesus was my pastor, I would surely tithe," but Hebrews 7:8 states:

That men (subject to death) receive tithes on this side; but on the other side, Jesus Himself receives them.

Why should we look for ways to excuse ourselves from what we know we should be doing? Let's be about establishing and not doing away with the words of our God. The tithe was, is and ever shall be holy unto the Lord.

Part II

Questions and Answers on Tithing

Introduction

After I wrote the original article on the tithe, I received hundreds of emails concerning this subject. Most of them were positive and encouraging, but not all. I realized then that I needed to address some of the major misconceptions people have about this all-important subject. Here are some of those misconceptions and my answers.

Pastor Eddie Cude

Misunderstanding #1

"The tithe was instituted under the Law, and since we are no longer under the Law, tithing is not for us today."

My Answer

The tithe came before the Law was given, and Abraham tithed unto Melchizedek (see Genesis 14:18-20). Tithing was required during the time of the Law (see Malachi 3:10). But tithing was also in effect after the Law (see Hebrews 5:6-7). Jesus is the Lord of the tithe forever, after the order of Melchizedek.

In Matthew 23:23, in the New Testament, Jesus plainly states that we should tithe and not leave the other (good works) undone. So, the tithe worked before the Law, it worked during the Law, and it is still working after the Law.

My question is this: If the tithe worked during the Law, what might it do under grace?

Misunderstanding #2

"Since tithing was under the Law and we are not under the Law anymore, we should not have to tithe."

My Answer

Under the Law, we were told, *"Thou shall not kill."* Would you kill someone today just because you are not under the Law anymore? Of course not. Don't check your brains at the door. If the tithe belongs to God, then Leviticus is right:

*The tithe is holy unto the L*ORD *and all the tithe of the land, whether of the seed of the land or of the fruit of the tress, it is the L*ORD*'s, it is holy unto the* L*ORD*.   Leviticus 27:30

Misunderstanding #3

"To avoid paying tithes prevents us from receiving a blessing. The tithe was given to us so that the blessing of God could enter this Earth."

My Answer

Who does not want the blessings of God? My question is: Why are so many people trying to keep the blessing of God out of this Earth?

The people who tithe don't get angry with those who don't tithe, but many who don't tithe attack those who do. Why is that?

Also, the person who is not saved (born again) will, many times, get "put out" with the one who is. One who has not been baptized in the Spirit of God gets upset with those who have been, and say that what they have experienced is not of God.

And so it is with people who do not tithe. They state that

tithing is not of God just because they don't personally tithe.

It is the same way with deliverance and divine healing. Those who have not received many times persecute those who have (see Galatians 4:28-29).

Let us cast off all excuses and obey God, that we might be blessed.

Misunderstanding #4

"Jesus gave us an eleventh commandment, that we should love the Lord with all our heart, mind and strength and love our neighbors as ourselves. He never said anything about accusing them. In fact, Revelation 12:11 states that Satan is *'the accuser of the brethren.'*"

My Answer

I have never heard of a born-again man or woman getting upset because a preacher ministers on being born again, and I have never heard a tither getting upset because a preacher ministers on the tithe. It is always those who do not tithe who get upset.

As I stated earlier, I am told that only twenty percent of Christians tithe regularly. If that is true, then fully eighty percent of all Christian feel uncomfortable with this subject.

I am thankful for those who stand for these truths. We must have a backbone enough to stand for what is right and not just go along with what the majority believe.

Jesus was not always popular with those in His day, and He said that we should tithe. Why can't we just take Him at His word?

The Scriptures state:

The letter kills, but the Spirit gives life.

Some people on both sides of his issue get very legalistic about it. One group insists that those who fail to tithe are under a curse, and the other group insists that tithing is no longer required, since we are now under grace. The real truth is that when applied with the right spirit and motivation, the tithe works every time and will produce blessings in your life.

In order to be blessed by God, we need:

1. Right motives

2. Right information, and

3. Right methods

These three things will guarantee that the promises of God in His Word will be yours because of your obedience to give, including the tithe.

Serving Him by Serving them,

Pastor Eddie Cude

About the Author

Eddie Cude and his wife, Bobbie, pastor a church in El Campo, Texas called El Campo Faith Center Church. He is an anointed servant of God in the five-fold ministry who is blessed with the gifts of the Holy Spirit operating in his ministry.

Pastor Cude is an outstanding teacher of the Word, and El Campo Faith Center Church is strong in evangelism and outreach ministries, serving as prayer partners and counselors to many other ministers.

Pastor Cude can be reached via e-mail at:

efc2@sbcglobal.net

www.ingramcontent.com/pod-product-compliance
Lightning Source LLC
Chambersburg PA
CBHW020526030426
42337CB00011B/557